A STORY OF JEAN

BY
SUSAN GAITSKELL

ILLUSTRATED BY
LAURIE LAFRANCE

TORONTO
OXFORD UNIVERSITY PRESS
1989

For Jessie,
on whose island it all began.
—S.G.

For my Mom
and The Old Trapper.
—L.L.

FOREWORD

This story tells about something that happened to me when I was a child in school. Because I was cross-eyed and because I was different in other ways, other kids chased me and called me hurtful names. I was frightened of them and I was sad because I wanted friends very much. But I was not lonely and afraid all the time. I played with my younger brother and sister. I went to the library and took home wonderful books to read. I learned, bit by bit, how to make friends with other children. One thing I was especially good at was telling stories. By the time I was ten, I knew I would like to be a writer some day.

In this book, Susan Gaitskell has told about the bad times. And she has shown how I was helped by my story-loving self. What happens to Jean in this story may not have happened exactly the way the book says it did. But it did really happen, all the same. Sometimes, in a poem or a story, you can make readers understand something real by showing it to them through imaginary characters. When I first read about Jean talking to the magical girl in the blue-flecked glasses, I thought, "Who is that girl? I don't remember her." Then I read on and I recognized that mysterious girl. She was just as real as the Jean who ran away from the bullies and lay face down on her bed, crying.

So, *A Story of Jean* is a made-up, true story. I hope you like it. I wonder if there is a Jean in your class. I think there is probably a Jean inside you. I am quite sure you will love going with her and her friends on their star journey. I did.

JEAN LITTLE

JEAN could see stars best when the sky was very black. She loved the stars. They lit the darkness with sparkles and brightened the night. Even when they disappeared, Jean knew they'd be back. She could count on the stars.

There was one that shone brighter than all the others. This was Jean's special star. She thought of it whenever she was lonely and she made up stories to make it laugh. She never told it sad stories because she was afraid that they might dull its sparkle. But Jean knew sad stories as well as she knew funny ones. Jean knew all sorts of stories.

She had tried to share her stories with the children at school, but that was difficult. Many of them just smirked and turned away from her. Others made jokes that hurt her feelings. It seemed that no one liked a girl who made up so many stories, particularly a girl who was almost blind, like Jean was.

Unless Jean pressed her nose against a book and stared, she couldn't see what was written on the page in front of her. Even while she stared, the words jumped everywhere. "Stand still," Jean told them, but it was no use. Words aren't like stars. They're hard to see when they twinkle.

One day, Jean was leaving the school yard with a story half-started in her head. Suddenly voices rang out from the shadows.

"Hey, Cross-eyes, there's ink all over your nose."

Jean stopped, terrified. She could barely see the faces of the children who were shouting at her; she could only hear their taunts.

She tried her best not to cry or run away, but shame brought tears to her eyes and fear made her feet turn for home.

"Cry baby, cry baby. Look at her run."

The faster Jean ran, the heavier the footsteps sounded behind her and the louder the voices shrilled. Jean ran so fast she fell, but she got up and ran some more. At last she crossed the doorstep of her house. She was safe.

That night Jean couldn't think of any stories to tell the stars. She turned her face to the wall and cried until sleep came.

At midnight she awoke. She thought she saw the shadow of a girl about her size. The girl was sitting cross-legged in the moonlight on Jean's window sill. She wore thick glasses with tiny flecks of blue in them — the same blue Jean had in her own eyes. The girl spoke.

"Too bad about today."

Jean looked at her suspiciously. "What do you know about today?" she asked.

"I was there," said the girl.

"I didn't see you," Jean replied.

"You weren't looking," said the girl.

But Jean was looking now and she could see the girl very clearly. She wasn't bouncing like words or twinkling like stars. She was just sitting there, staring at Jean.

Jean stared back, straight into the girl's thick glasses.

''Wait a minute,'' Jean exclaimed suddenly. ''You're blind! You're as blind as I am.''

''Not quite,'' said the girl. ''I saw something you didn't see today.''

''Humph,'' Jean grunted out loud. Who did this blind kid think she was?

Jean pulled up the bedcovers and pretended to snore. But soon she opened her eyes again, just a crack. The girl was gone.

"Now I'll never know what she saw," sighed Jean sadly. "Well, who cares?" But Jean cared. She cared so much that she couldn't stop thinking about the girl no matter how hard she tried. Jean got out of bed and went to the window. She looked around the sky and found her special star. Then she made a wish.

At that moment her star began to grow.

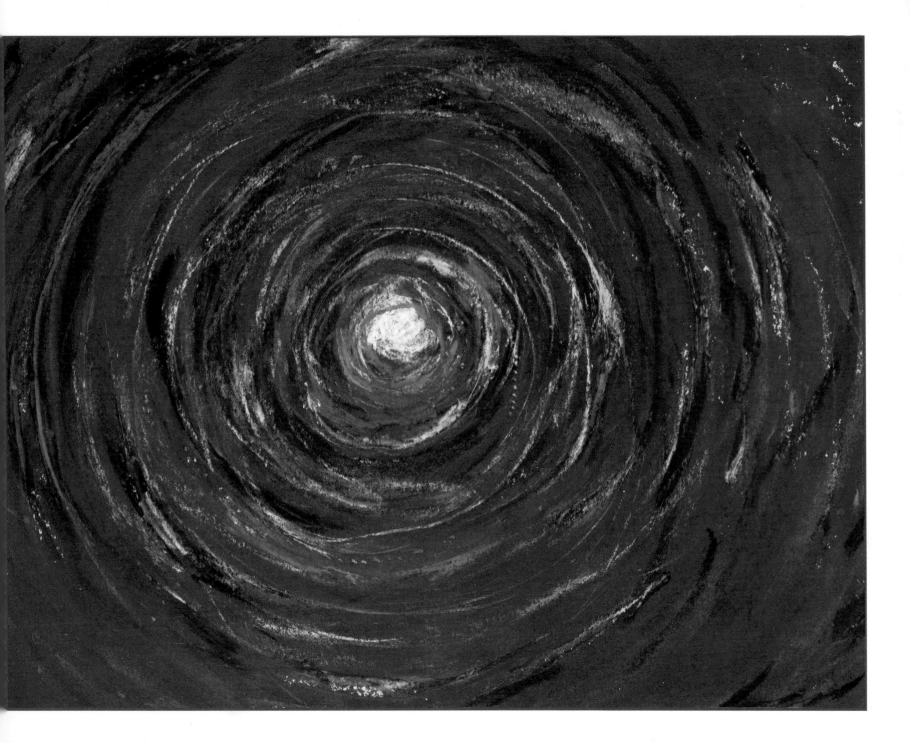

It grew and grew until it was so huge that it touched her window. It was bright white and on it, holding out her hand to Jean, was the girl with the blue-flecked glasses.

"Come for a ride," said the girl. And, without looking back, Jean stepped onto the star and rode into the night.

As the star sped farther and farther into the darkness, Jean remembered a funny story she'd made up a long time ago. She told it out loud and the stars shimmered with laughter. The girl with the blue-flecked glasses laughed too.

Jean stared proudly at the girl. "I bet your stories can't make the sky laugh," she said.

"No, but they can make your heart sing," said the girl. And she began to fill the night with stories about best friends and birthdays and long afternoons by the sea. Jean knew these stories well because she'd heard them in her own heart. For a long time she'd kept them there, secretly, because even starlight, she feared, might fade them.

"Your stories are mine," Jean said to the girl, who nodded and clasped Jean's hand in hers.

The star glided downwards toward the earth. As it dropped through the night, Jean heard the sound of singing deep in the sky. It matched the sound her heart made.

The more Jean listened, the stronger her heart sounds grew and the fainter the music of the sky became, until at last the singing was inside her.

The star dropped faster toward the earth. Jean felt a rush of cold air on her cheeks. She and the girl with the blue-flecked glasses were flying into a darker sound. Fearful and loud, it shrilled in Jean's ears and shivered through her spine.

"What is this?" Jean screamed.

"Open your eyes and look," said the girl.

For a second Jean did open her eyes. When she saw the school yard, she closed them again, tightly.

"Take me away," Jean shouted. "Why did you bring me here?"

"To see what you wouldn't see before," answered the girl.

Jean looked everywhere but in the direction of the shouting.

"Look, Jean. You must look," said the girl, and she put her hand on Jean's shoulder and pointed to the place that Jean feared the most.

Jean opened her eyes. She saw mouths gaping, fingers jabbing, faces leering, all turned toward her. She saw the shadow of herself run away. Everything was just as it had been this morning.

But now, beyond the blur of the faces, she saw something else. There was one boy who was not shouting. He was trembling as a single tear dropped onto his cheek. A long way off stood a girl whose eyes were wide with horror. Another, standing alone in the crowd, covered her ears with her hands and looked away.

"What about them, Jean? Who's going to tell stories for them?" asked the girl with the blue-flecked glasses.

At that moment Jean knew that she was. She felt what they felt. She saw what they saw, but she felt it more strongly and she saw it more clearly than they could.

Jean jumped off her star and marched past the jeering and through the shouting.

Jean found the three children who were alone and gathered them together.

"Come for a ride," she said. She helped them onto the star and the shouting began to fade.

As they rode into the night together, Jean glanced back, just once, at the crowd of children. The night was dark, but she thought she saw an even darker shadow flickering across the faces they were leaving behind. The fierceness was gone. Some looked confused, some lonely, some afraid.

Jean turned to the children on the star and she began to tell them a story about themselves. It was funny and sad, bold and gentle, all at the same time. It made the children forget their fear, because Jean had forgotten hers. They listened to Jean until dawn broke. Then the star brought them home together.

After that, Jean and the girl with the blue-flecked glasses went back to that school yard and to others like it. They took many children for rides through the night and brought them safely home. Jean told all the stories she knew—even the sad ones—and the star they rode on grew brighter and brighter. By its light, Jean and the girl saw parts of the world and the sky they had never seen before. Jean made up so many stories that she couldn't remember them all, so she began to write down the ones she liked best.

Years have passed since Jean's first ride on the star. Through all those years, she and the girl with the blue-flecked glasses have never been far apart. Jean still tells stories and she still looks at stars. Her stories, like the stars, still brighten the night for those who see their magic.

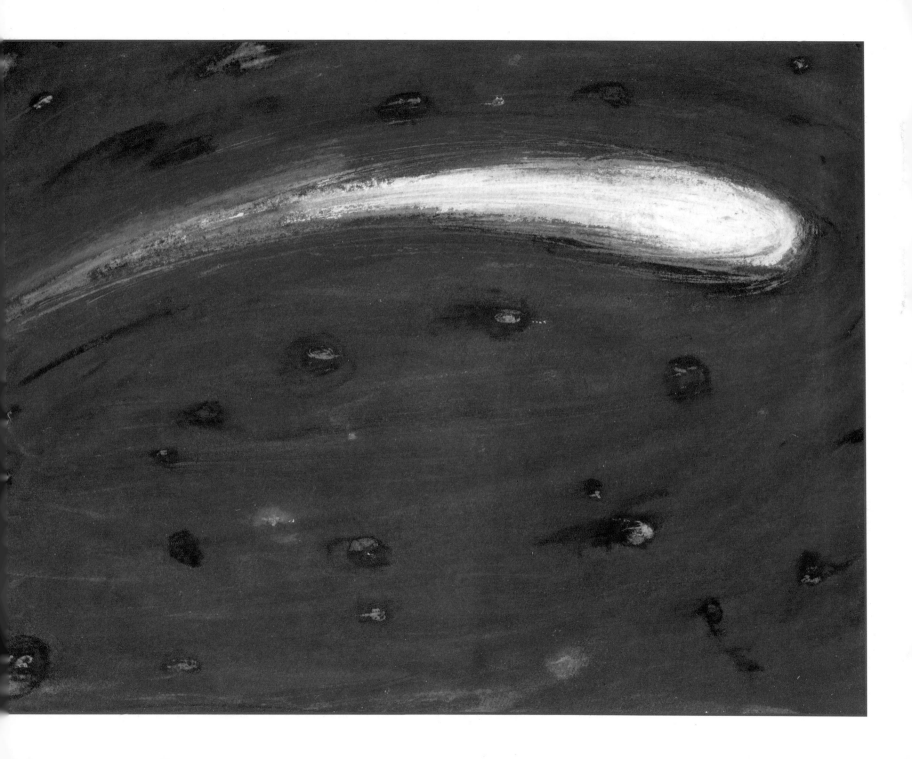

Oxford University Press, 70 Wynford Drive, Don Mills, Ontario, M3C 1J9

Toronto   Oxford   New York   Delhi   Bombay   Calcutta   Madras   Karachi
Petaling Jaya   Singapore   Hong Kong   Tokyo   Nairobi   Dar es Salaam
Cape Town   Melbourne   Auckland

and associated companies in
Berlin   Ibadan

Canadian Cataloguing in Publication Data
Gaitskell, Susan
A Story of Jean

ISBN 0-19-540736-9

1. Little, Jean, 1932–   —Biography—Youth—
Juvenile literature. 2. Novelists, Canadian
(English)—20th century—Biography—Juvenile literature.
3. Visually handicapped—Canada—Biography—
Juvenile literature.   I. Lafrance, Laurie, 1960–
II. Title.

PS8563.A338S86 1989   jC813'.54   C89-090073-6
PR9199.3.G34St 1989

Text © Susan Gaitskell 1989
Illustrations © Laurie Lafrance 1989

Oxford is a trademark of Oxford University Press
1 2 3 4 — 2 1 0 9
Printed in Hong Kong